Rumpelstiltskin
The True Story

by Stacey Sparks
illustrated by Linda Graves

Scott Foresman

Editorial Offices: Glenview, Illinois • New York, New York
Sales Offices: Reading, Massachusetts • Duluth, Georgia
Glenview, Illinois • Carrollton, Texas • Menlo Park, California

My name is Rumpelstiltskin.
"Boo! Hiss!" you growl?

I see you have already heard
of me. You may not like me. But
let me tell you my own side of
the story.

"Your first baby?" I asked.
"Fine!" she said.
So I spun every bit of straw into gold.
It was not easy! Have you ever tried to spin wet straw?

The prince saw the gold. He was
so happy! He married the girl. One
year later, they had a baby.

The princess was surprised when
I popped up again. I don't know
why. She had made me a promise.

"Please," she begged. "Don't take my baby!"

"Try to guess my name. If you do, I will not take him," I said.

Wasn't that nice of me?

"Jim? Pete? Joe?" she tried.
"No, my name is long," I said.
"Tom? John? Will?" she asked.
I told you she was silly.

"I'll give you one more day," I said.
The baby started to cry.
Why did I want this baby anyway?
He was much too loud.

That night I made a fire in a field
by a brook. I sang a song.
"Soon I'll win this little game.
Rumpelstiltskin is my name!" I sang.
Then I saw something jump up
and run away.

   The next day, the princess asked
if my name was Jake or Ed.
   "No," I said. I reached for the baby.
   "Is it . . . Rumpelstiltskin?"
   "Yes," I said with a growl.

So, the man lied to the prince. The prince was greedy. And the princess spied on me.

Why does everyone think I'm the bad guy in this story? I don't want to brag. But I think I'm the best of the bunch.

That is Right, Walrus

by Kana Riley

❀

illustrated by
Mircea Catusanu

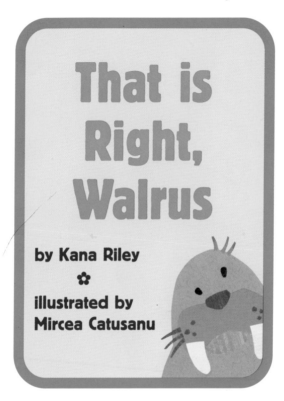

Scott Foresman

Editorial Offices: Glenview, Illinois • New York, New York
Sales Offices: Reading, Massachusetts • Duluth, Georgia
Glenview, Illinois • Carrollton, Texas • Menlo Park, California

Walrus is going to the beach.

What will she buy?
A snowsuit or a bathing suit?

No, no, Walrus.
That is not right.

Yes, Walrus!
That is right.

Walrus is going to a ranch.

What will she buy?
Skis or cowboy boots?

No, no, Walrus!
That is not right.

Yes, Walrus!
That is right.

Walrus is going camping.

What will she buy?
A bed or a sleeping bag?

No, no, Walrus!
That is not right.

12

Yes, Walrus!
That is right.

Walrus is going to see
Grandma.

What will she buy?
A book or flowers?

Yes, yes, Walrus.
They are both right!